WITHDRAWN

21st
Century
Skills Library

COOL SCIENCE CAREERS

FORENSIC PSYCHOLOGIST

Ann Heinrichs

Cherry Lake Publishing
Ann Arbor, Michigan

CHERRY LAKE
Publishing

Published in the United States of America by Cherry Lake Publishing
Ann Arbor, Michigan
www.cherrylakepublishing.com

Content Adviser: Mary W. Lindahl, Chair, Department of Forensic Psychology,
Marymount University

Photo Credits: Cover and page 1, ©Corbis Premium RF/Alamy; page 4, ©David R. Frazier
Photolibrary, Inc./Alamy; page 6, ©Ilene MacDonald/Alamy; page 8, ©Christina Kennedy/
Alamy; page 11, ©Mary Evans Picture Library/Alamy; page 13, ©Jupiterimages/Comstock
Images; pages 14 and 19, ©Mikael Karlsson/Alamy; page 20, ©iStockphoto.com/njgphoto;
page 24, ©iStockphoto.com/jpmediainc; page 26, ©Glow Images/Alamy

Library of Congress Cataloging-in-Publication Data

Heinrichs, Ann.
 Forensic psychologist / by Ann Heinrichs.
    p. cm.—(Cool science careers)
 Includes index.
 ISBN-13: 978-1-60279-309-5
 ISBN-10: 1-60279-309-3
 1. Forensic psychology—Juvenile literature. 2. Forensic psychology—
Vocational guidance—Juvenile literature. I. Title.
 RA1148.H47 2008
 614'.15—dc22   2008029291

Cherry Lake Publishing would like to acknowledge the work of
The Partnership for 21st Century Skills.
Please visit www.21stcenturyskills.org for more information.

TABLE OF CONTENTS

CHAPTER ONE

PSYCHOLOGY MEETS THE LAW

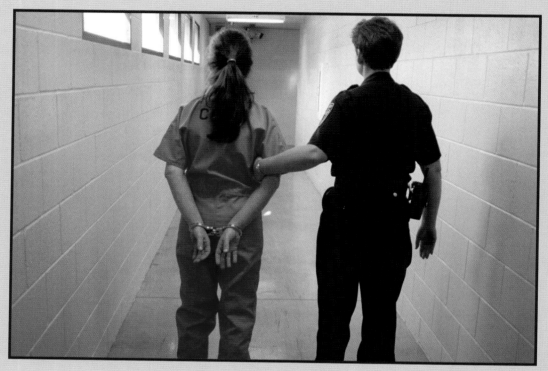

Guards help make sure that inmates are not a danger to forensic psychologists when they visit prisons.

Cliff is in jail, accused of murder. A forensic psychologist is asking him questions. Cliff's eyes are not focusing very well. He fidgets and cannot seem to pay attention. Suddenly, he leaps out of his chair and starts screaming wildly. Is he suffering from a mental illness? Or is he faking it? That's up to the forensic psychologist to figure out. Cliff's future hangs on the answer. He could spend the rest of his life in prison. Or he could go to a **psychiatric** hospital, where he'll get treatment and care.

This scene is one of many that may occur in a forensic psychologist's career. That career combines two fields of study: psychology and forensic science. A psychologist studies how people behave and how their minds work. A forensic scientist uses science to solve legal questions or issues involving the law. Forensic psychologists are experts who weave together psychology and the law. They use their psychology skills to serve the legal system.

Often, the forensic psychologist can help determine the mental state of a **defendant** at the time of the crime. A defendant's mental condition can also be a factor in deciding whether he or she is fit to stand **trial**. In a way, forensic psychologists are like detectives. To arrive at the

It is important for forensic psychologists to present their findings clearly and accurately. Their expert opinions can greatly influence the outcome of the cases they work on.

facts, they ask all kinds of questions related to mental and legal issues.

Does the accused person understand the crime? Is the person able to take part in a trial? Is he or she mentally ill, or just pretending? Does the person know the difference between right and wrong? All these questions are important in determining the responsibility of a criminal.

When it's time for a trial, the forensic psychologist may appear in court. Here, a judge is in charge of the proceedings. Two sides present facts about the crime. On one side is the prosecutor. The prosecutor represents the government during legal proceedings. Prosecutors try to prove that the accused is guilty. On the other side is the defendant. His or her lawyer wants to show that the defendant is not guilty.

Both sides may call **witnesses** to testify, or report what they know. Forensic psychologists are known as **expert witnesses**. They have special knowledge and skills that

21st Century Content

In 1843, an Englishman named Daniel M'Naghten was accused of murder. A jury found him not guilty by reason of insanity. The British government reviewed this decision. They decided defendants who don't understand the nature of their crime or that what they did was wrong can use the insanity defense. This is now known as the M'Naghten rule.

In the United States, different states handle the insanity defense in different ways. In many states, a defendant can be found not guilty by reason of insanity. Idaho, Montana, and Utah have done away with the insanity defense altogether. In those states, a defendant can be declared "guilty but insane." Today, the insanity defense is used in very few court cases. It is not often successful.

Stay informed. How does your state government handle the insanity defense?

Forensic psychologists who work with children face special challenges. They must make sure a child feels comfortable during an interview.

shed light on the case. The members of the jury listen to all the witnesses. They use the information to make a decision: guilty or not guilty.

The forensic psychologist may be asked to help with other decisions, too. If the defendant is found guilty, part of his or her **sentence** may involve treatment in a **rehabilitation** or psychiatric program. The forensic psychologist may even oversee these programs. How likely is the person to commit the crime again? What kind of treatment does he or she need? These questions involve both psychology and the law.

Many people think forensic psychologists deal only with criminal cases. But many other legal issues may require their services. In divorce cases, which parent should the children live with? Does an elderly person understand decisions about his or her care? Did a workplace accident damage a person's mental ability? These questions also involve psychology and the law.

The first recorded instance of a psychologist taking part in a trial was in 1896. A man in Germany was accused of three murders. Stories about the crimes were splashed across newspapers as the trial approached. The stories were full of details and reports from various people.

At the trial, many witnesses said they saw the murders and described what they saw. Then psychologist Albert von Schrenk-Notzing was called as an expert witness. He had done research on how memory works. He said the witnesses couldn't tell the difference between what they really saw and what they had read in the newspapers. Legal experts today still argue about how reliable **eyewitnesses** are.

Psychologist William Stern began studying memory in 1901. He found that memories are often not accurate. As more time passed after an event, people remembered fewer details or made errors when recalling the details. Stern also found that certain kinds of questions could produce false memories. For example, he might ask "Did you see the man with the knife?" That's called a leading question because it leads the person toward a specific answer. The person might say yes, even if the man had no knife. Stern's studies shed more light on eyewitness reports.

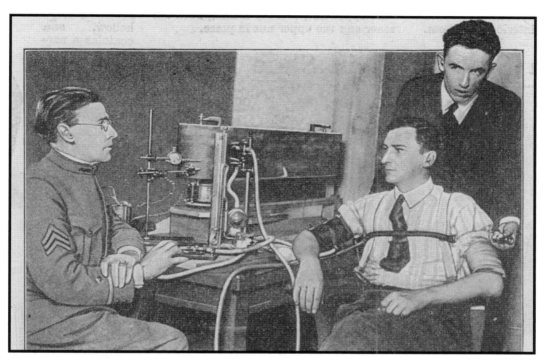

People have questioned the reliability of the lie detector throughout the device's history. Today, experts realize that many factors can affect the test's results.

Hugo Münsterberg published his book *On the Witness Stand* in 1908. It argued that many psychological factors are involved in criminal cases. By 1917, psychologist William Marston suggested that when people are lying, their **blood pressure** is likely to rise. This led to the invention of the modern polygraph, or lie detector. Polygraph test results cannot be used in most courts, though. Psychologists disagree about whether polygraphs are reliable. But they are still sometimes used in police investigations.

For years, medical doctors were considered better expert witnesses than psychologists. In 1940, courts ruled that expert witnesses must have a lot of knowledge about the subject they testify on. Medical doctors don't necessarily have much knowledge of psychology. Gradually, psychologists gained more acceptance in the legal system.

Today, thousands of people work as forensic psychologists. Their job is often stressful and, in extreme cases, dangerous. But being a forensic psychologist can be very satisfying.

CHAPTER TWO

WORKING AS A FORENSIC PSYCHOLOGIST

Lawyers are just some of the many people forensic psychologists might work with while evaluating a defendant.

A forensic psychologist may begin the day by consulting a defendant's lawyer. The lawyer wants the forensic psychologist to examine the defendant. But first, the lawyer shares background information on the person. That might include police reports, any criminal history, earlier

Defendants may not want to discuss their past or the crime. A good forensic psychologist is able to get a defendant to open up and talk.

psychological reports, medical records, past behavior, and family history. Now, the forensic psychologist is ready to face the defendant. It's time to visit the jail.

A guard meets the forensic psychologist, and they proceed through winding hallways. The forensic psychologist must remain calm and focus on the job ahead. At last, they reach an interview room. The defendant is brought in. The forensic psychologist questions the defendant while the guard remains nearby.

Defendants are usually asked to explain what happened before, during, and after the crime. They are asked why they did it and what they were thinking and feeling at the time. Other questions may cover the person's early life, family and friends, jobs, drug and alcohol abuse, physical abuse, or medical problems. Throughout this entire process, the forensic psychologist watches for lies or **deceptive** behavior.

Then the forensic psychologist studies information from the interview and all other sources. He or she may consult various resources, too. One useful book is the *Diagnostic and Statistical Manual of Mental Disorders*, or *DSM* for short. It's a standard manual used to help **diagnose** mental problems. *Psychological Evaluations for the Courts: A Handbook for Mental Health Professionals and Lawyers* is

a must-have for forensic psychologists, too. Books that define crimes and explain the law are also valuable. The forensic psychologist must have a clear understanding of these subjects.

Gradually, the forensic psychologist forms an expert opinion about the defendant's mental condition and provides a detailed report. At the trial, the forensic psychologist presents his or her professional opinion, making sure to explain things clearly so everyone can understand. Forensic psychologists must also be able to back up what they say and explain how they arrived at their opinions.

Forensic psychologists sometimes help in civil cases, too. Those are cases that do not involve criminal charges. For example, suppose a woman is injured in a car accident. She claims she has suffered brain damage. She wants the guilty driver to pay her a lot of money because of her injury. A forensic psychologist would examine the woman to see if her claims are true.

Forensic psychologists also help resolve family court issues such as child **custody**. In these cases, a child's parents are getting divorced and are going to live in separate homes. The court needs to decide where the child should live. The forensic psychologist visits both homes, questions each parent, and looks around. Is the home a nice place for children to live? How do the parent and child get along?

Often, the most important information comes from the child. Where does he or she want to live, and why? Sometimes the homes of other family members are considered for custody. Finally, the forensic psychologist reports an opinion to the court.

Forensic psychologists may be asked to evaluate reports of child abuse. They meet with both adults and children to gather information. They try to determine any patterns of abuse. They may also recommend ways to deal with specific cases, including removing the child from the abusive situation.

Forensic psychologists may provide services for police departments, hospitals, colleges and universities, or community mental health centers. Or they may have their own private practices.

A forensic psychologist may also visit juvenile detention facilities. These are places where young people accused of crimes are held. Many times, they must stay there until they reach adulthood. In most states, that is defined as age 18. Many young lawbreakers have psychological problems. Often **counseling** is more beneficial for them than prison. A forensic psychologist interviews the young

Forensic psychologists who specialize in treating juvenile inmates know how to deal with teenagers.

person. School records, family situations, and past criminal activities are also reviewed. The forensic psychologist's report helps the court decide on the best plan for the young person. This decision can mean the difference between going to a juvenile detention facility or receiving rehabilitation services.

CHAPTER THREE

BECOMING A FORENSIC PSYCHOLOGIST

Forensic psychologists review a lot of information when evaluating cases.

Are you considering a career in forensic psychology? If so, you will need a lot of education and experience. But the best forensic psychologists have certain personal qualities, too. These traits can be just as important for a successful career.

Forensic psychologists should have a real desire to help others. Good psychologists are patient. They hold back judgments and try to understand people and their motivations. They are comfortable working with many different kinds of people and are open to a variety of situations and experiences. A forensic psychologist should also be good at speaking in public. This is useful when testifying in court.

Many forensic psychologists are licensed clinical psychologists. A clinical psychologist can work with individual patients, families, or groups. To become licensed, a psychologist must have a doctoral degree. That requires three steps. The amount of time required to earn different degrees varies from program to program and school to school. First comes a bachelor's degree, which usually takes four years of college. Next comes a master's degree, which usually takes two more years. Finally, a doctoral degree generally requires three or more years after that.

Some forensic psychologists help with criminal profiling. This involves analyzing the scene of a crime to learn about the person who did it. Based on the way the crime was committed, the profiler develops ideas about the criminal's sex, age, ethnic group, and personality. Criminal profilers are heroic figures in movies and TV shows. In real life, however, job opportunities are rare. Most police departments hardly ever use profilers. They prefer standard methods of investigating crimes. Many scholars don't believe that profiling qualifies as a real science.

Forensic psychologists who do profiling work must be able to analyze and make sense of different pieces of evidence and information. They use this information to form a description of a criminal. What are some other skills that criminal profilers should have?

For your bachelor's degree, psychology is a good choice for a major. Some colleges even have a major in forensic psychology. Classes about mental health law and court procedures are useful, too. With a bachelor's degree in psychology or forensic psychology, you might work as a youth counselor or drug abuse counselor. These jobs involve both psychology and the law.

Master's degree students get a lot of experience working with patients. With a master's degree in clinical psychology, you might work in a prison or a mental health facility. With a nonclinical degree, different opportunities are open to you. Instead of working with patients, you might do research in forensic psychology.

As a doctoral student, you spend even more time with patients. Finally, after earning a doctoral degree in clinical psychology, you must pass a state exam. Then you receive a license to practice psychology in that state. Some people also take a licensing exam from the American Board of Forensic Psychology. Although taking the licensing exam may be beneficial, it is not required to work in the field.

As a licensed forensic psychologist, you might join the staff of a psychiatric hospital. Or you can open your own private office. You might specialize in dealing with issues involving young offenders, adult criminals, or family law. Your specialty could be counseling, advising lawyers, or serving as an expert witness. These are some of the many ways you can combine psychology and the law.

CHAPTER FOUR

EMERGING ISSUES, GROWING NEEDS

Should an older person live alone? As the population ages, forensic psychologists may find themselves answering more questions involving legal issues and the elderly.

Forensic psychology is a field that's growing fast. Legal issues are changing all the time. Researchers in psychology are making new discoveries. And new trends are being discovered in people's behavior patterns. All these factors create a higher demand for forensic psychologists.

For example, certain types of violent behavior are on the rise. In the late 20th century and into the 21st century, a series of shocking mass shootings made headlines. Such shootings can take place in schools or workplaces. Some occur in malls, department stores, or restaurants. What makes people commit these deadly acts? How can they be prevented? Psychology researchers will continue to seek answers to these questions.

Family law faces increasing challenges, too. Divorced parents often live hundreds or thousands of miles apart. This gives forensic psychologists more factors to consider in child custody cases.

Harassment and **discrimination** are also growing issues. More victims are now speaking up instead of keeping quiet. The law recognizes that these offenses may cause psychological suffering. Courts can require offenders to pay victims. In these cases, a forensic psychologist is

Do you think kids should be allowed to serve as witnesses in court?

called in. He or she must determine the seriousness of the victim's psychological injury.

Forensic psychologists continue their research on memory. They hope to learn more about an eyewitness's ability to recall events. Children's memories are a rich subject for research, too. It is a common belief that a child's memory is less reliable than an adult's. It is true that a child may be influenced by suggestions or leading questions from unskilled interviewers. But it's becoming clear that even young kids will resist being misled if their memories are strong enough. Can children be reliable witnesses in court? Further research will shed more light on this question.

Researchers are also learning more about brain injuries. These injuries might come from car accidents, workplace accidents, or physical fights. Such injuries can result in the loss of jobs or homes.

Learning & Innovation Skills

Some defendants pretend to suffer from mental conditions such as amnesia, or loss of memory. They may say they can't remember their crimes or even their own names. Forensic psychologists often use the Rey Visual Memory Test to determine amnesia. The subject looks at a card with 15 common symbols. After viewing each symbol for a set amount of time, the person is asked to recall as many of those symbols as possible. Studies have shown that even people with severe brain damage can recall at least eight symbols. But a defendant who's faking amnesia may produce only two or three symbols. Busted!

Experts work hard to come up with improved and creative tests that make it difficult for people to influence the results by being dishonest. Why do you think someone accused of a crime would pretend to have amnesia?

With a deeper understanding of brain damage, a forensic psychologist can evaluate the injury and its effects.

At one time, psychology had little or very limited influence in the legal system. Today, we realize that criminal behavior—and human behavior in general—is complex. To deal with these issues fairly, we need sensitivity and scientific insight. That's why psychology entered the legal system. And it's here to stay.

Some Famous Forensic Psychologists

William Marston (1893–1947) was an American psychologist who developed the use of a blood pressure test to detect lying. This eventually led to the invention of the polygraph, often called the lie detector test. He also is known for creating the Wonder Woman comic book character.

Hugo Münsterberg (1863–1916) was a German psychologist who applied his work to law, industry, and medicine. His 1908 book *On the Witness Stand* called for psychologists to be used in criminal cases.

William Stern (1871–1938) was a German psychologist. His 1901 studies on memory revealed how faulty memories can be. He applied these studies to determine how reliable eyewitnesses are. He also invented the intelligence quotient (IQ) as a way to establish a person's mental abilities.

Michael Stone (1933–) is a forensic psychiatrist who studies murderers. He developed a "scale of evil," rating murderers from 1 to 22. He hosts the Investigation Discovery channel's TV show *Most Evil*.

Lewis Terman (1877–1956) was a psychologist and professor at California's Stanford University. He helped introduce the Stanford-Binet intelligence test. In 1916, he began using this test on people applying to be police officers.

Lenore Walker (1942–) is a forensic psychologist who specializes in domestic abuse cases. She is the director of the Domestic Violence Institute and has written many books.

Michael Welner (1964–) is a forensic psychiatrist and expert on criminal behavior. In 1998, he founded The Forensic Panel to establish objective standards among forensic psychologists and psychiatrists.

GLOSSARY

blood pressure (BLUHD PRESH-ur) the force of blood pushing against the walls of blood vessels

counseling (KOUN-suhl-eeng) meetings to provide help with personal or psychological problems

custody (KUSS-tuh-dee) the legal right to care for a child

deceptive (di-SEP-tiv) misleading, or giving a false or confusing impression

defendant (di-FEN-duhnt) someone who is accused of a crime

diagnose (dye-uhg-NOHSS) to identify a patient's illness or disorder

discrimination (dis-krim-uh-NAY-shuhn) unfair treatment due to race, sex, age, religion, or other factors

expert witnesses (EX-purt WIT-niss-ez) people with special knowledge or skills who testify at a trial

eyewitnesses (eye-WIT-niss-ez) people who claim they saw a crime or event take place

harassment (huh-RASS-muhnt) unwanted verbal or physical actions that threaten or bother someone

psychiatric (sye-kee-AT-rik) related to mental disorders

rehabilitation (ree-uh-bih-luh-TAY-shuhn) training to help a sick or injured person return to health

sentence (SEN-tuhnss) the punishment given to a person found guilty of a crime in court

trial (TRY-uhl) an examination of the facts and evidence about a crime, presented before a judge and jury

witnesses (WIT-niss-ez) people who testify and give evidence at a trial

FOR MORE INFORMATION

Books

Beres, D. B. *Killer at Large: Criminal Profilers and the Cases They Solve!* New York: Scholastic, 2007.

Esherick, Joan. *Criminal Psychology and Personality Profiling.* Broomall, PA: Mason Crest Publishers, 2006.

Web Sites

American Board of Forensic Psychology: Brochure
www.abfp.com/brochure.asp
Learn more about what forensic psychologists do

Forensic Science: Psychological Profiling
http://library.thinkquest.org/04oct/00206/nts_psychological_profiling.htm
Read about the practice of psychological profiling

United States Attorneys Kids Page: Courtroom Staff
www.usdoj.gov/usao/eousa/kidspage/courtroom_personnel.html
Check out the layout of a courtroom, and learn about some of the many people who participate in trials

INDEX

ABOUT THE AUTHOR

Ann Heinrichs is the author of more than 200 books for children and young adults. They cover U.S. and world history and culture, science and nature, and English grammar. Ann has also enjoyed careers as a children's book editor and an advertising copywriter. An avid traveler, she has toured Europe, Africa, the Middle East, and East Asia. Born in Fort Smith, Arkansas, she now lives in Chicago. She enjoys biking, kayaking, and flying kites.